LINES ON THE UNDERGROUND

an anthology
for Piccadilly Line travellers

Compiled by

DOROTHY MEADE & TATIANA WOLFF

Illustrated by Basil Cottle
and Jonathan Newdick

CASSELL

Cassell Publishers Limited
Wellington House, 125 Strand
London WC2R 0BB

in association with the London Transport Museum

Selection
copyright © Dorothy Meade and Tatiana Wolff 1994, 1996
Extracts copyright authors and publishers (see Acknowledgements)
Illustrations copyright © Basil Cottle and Jonathan Newdick 1994

This edition published 1996
The material in this anthology was first published in
Lines on the Underground, 1994

British Library Cataloguing in Publication Data
A catalogue record for this book is available from the British Library

ISBN 0-304-34839-2

Distributed in Australia by
Capricorn Link (Australia) Pty Ltd
2/13 Carrington Road, Castle Hill, NSW 2154

Printed and bound in Great Britain by Hillman Printers Ltd

To Joe, Dora, Anna and Ben

*

And in memory of
M. M. W.

Heathrow Terminal 4

Last night in London Airport
I saw a wooden bin
labelled UNWANTED LITERATURE
IS TO BE PLACED HEREIN.
So I wrote a poem
and popped it in.

CHRISTOPHER LOGUE, 'Last Night in London Airport',
Ode to the Dodo: Poems 1953–1978, 1981

Heathrow Terminals 1, 2, 3

It never failed to surprise [Margaret] that in all the years we had been travelling . . . the control officers at Heathrow had never raised an eyebrow as they stamped her passport. Yet, as she had often remarked, 'I'll bet I'm the only person using this beastly airport that was actually born right here right underneath the control tower!'

Which was not strictly true. For when she was born there was no control tower, no airport – just the ancient farmhouse that was her home, lying at the core of its surrounding orchards and fields. . . .

Most of the land was given over to orchards – Morello cherries . . . apples and plums.

Most weekdays, long before dawn, some of the great shire horses were harnessed to the firm's massive canary-yellow carts to take the loads of fruit and flowers to the [family's] stall in Covent Garden.

MARGARET AND ALICK POTTER, *Everything is Possible*, 1984

Hatton Cross

On 16 December 1977 Her Majesty the Queen rode in the cab of a special train from Hatton Cross to Heathrow Central and unveiled a memorial plaque. The Heathrow extension was both officially open and open to the public. Air travellers began to 'Fly the Tube' the same day, the first of 12 million eventually expected to use the line every year.

JOHN R. DAY, *The Story of London's Underground*, 1963

Hounslow West

Return'd with my Lord by Hounslow Heath, where we saw the newly-rais'd army encamp'd, design'd against France, in pretence at least, but which gave umbrage to the Parliament. His Majesty and a world of company were in the field, and the whole army in battalia: a very glorious sight. Now were brought into service a new sort of Soldiers called Granadiers, who were dextrous in flinging hand granados, every one having a pouchfull; they had furr'd caps with coped crownes, like Janizaries, which made them look very fierce, and some had long hoods hanging down behind, as we picture fools. Their clothing being likewise pybald yellow and red.

JOHN EVELYN, *Diary, 29 June 1678*

As far back as about 1650 [Hounslow] was noted for its numerous inns and ale-houses. . . .

At the accession of Queen Victoria there were as many as five hundred stage-coaches and one thousand five hundred horses daily employed in transit through the town.

E. WALFORD, *Greater London*, 1882–4

Sir,
. . . In the early morning mist, in the early 1940s, six boys from a west London grammar school would assemble at Hounslow West Station – at that time the end of the Piccadilly line . . . and equipped with an Underground map and red pencil, we would 'travel the tracks'. . . . We could be back at Hounslow Central sufficiently early in the evening to avoid arousing parental suspicion.
Yours sincerely,
James Mogford

Letter to *The Times*, 19 February 1994

Hounslow Central

Hounslow Heath is a sample of all that is bad in soil, and villainous in look.

WILLIAM COBBETT, *Rural Rides*, 1830

Celebrated 'powder mills' at North Feltham . . . some of the first gunpowder made in England was manufactured here. It was chancy stuff: the explosions, which occurred every few months, terrified Middlesex residents for two centuries. Horace Walpole complained about one which in 1772, damaged parts of his house at Strawberry Hill.

BRUCE STEVENSON, *Middlesex*, 1972

Hounslow East

You have read of my calamity without knowing it, and will pity me when you do. I have been blown up; my castle is blown up; Guy Fawkes has been about my house; and the 5th of November has fallen on the 6th of January! In short, nine thousand powder-mills broke loose yesterday morning on Hounslow-heath; a whole squadron of them came hither, and have broken eight of my painted-glass windows; and the north side of the castle looks as if it had stood a siege. The two saints of the hall have suffered martyrdom! they have had their bodies cut off, and nothing remains but their heads. . . . As the storm came from the north-west, the china-closet was not touched, not a cup fell down. The bow-window of brave old coloured glass, at Mr. Hindley's, is massacred; and all the north sides of Twickenham and Brentford are shattered. At London, it was proclaimed an earthquake, and half the inhabitants ran into the street.

HORACE WALPOLE, letter to the Hon. H.S. Conway, 7 January 1772

Osterley

Osterley House is magnificent. . . . Gresham, its original owner, was ostentatious. When Elizabeth I visited him here in 1576 she criticised the proportions of the courtyard. So Sir Thomas, overnight, had a wall built down the middle of it: 'It was questionable,' wrote Thomas Fuller, 'whether the Queen was more contented with the conformity to her fancy, or more pleased with the surprise and the sudden performance thereof.'

BRUCE STEVENSON, *Middlesex*, 1972

On Friday we went to see – oh, the palace of palaces! [Osterley House] – and yet a palace *sans crown, sans coronet*, but such expense! such taste! such profusion! . . . The old house I have often seen, which was built by Sir Thomas Gresham; but it is so improved and enriched, that all the Percies and Seymours of Syon must die of envy . . . a drawing-room worthy of Eve before the Fall. Mrs. Child's dressing-room is full of pictures, gold filigree, china and japan. So is all the house; the chairs are taken from antique lyres, and make charming harmony. . . . Not to mention a kitchen-garden that costs 1400 l. a-year, a menagerie full of birds that come from a thousand islands . . . and then the Park is – the ugliest spot of ground in the universe – and so I returned comforted to Strawberry.

HORACE WALPOLE, letter to the Countess of Ossory, 21 June 1773

Boston Manor

Boston Manor House at Brentford is a fine Tudor/Jacobean building said to be haunted by a Lady Boston who was killed by her husband when he found her *in flagrante delicto* with another man. He was successful in keeping her death secret, burying her body in the park. Her ladyship glides shadow-like from the back of the house along a path leading to a great cypress tree, where she disappears. A lady in white, who drowned herself in the lake after an unhappy love-affair, also haunts the lawns at the back of the house.

J.A. BROOKS, *Ghosts of London*, 1982

Northfields

Charles Blondin the tightrope walker lived here; there is no plaque, but Niagara House, a block of flats in Northfield Avenue, may remind the passer-by of one of his exploits.

BRUCE STEVENSON, *Middlesex*, 1972

South Ealing

Turn to page 10 for Acton Town

The manor of Ealing [or as it was sometimes written Yealing, Yelling, or Yeling] has belonged to the See of London from the earliest times.

E. WALFORD, *Greater London*, 1882–4

While we were away in Yorkshire my sister was born. My brother Cyril and I were silenced by this incomprehensible piece of news. Were our parents not satisfied with us? No sooner are we in Ealing than there is another baby, my youngest brother. Another betrayal. Why clutter up the place? It happens on my birthday, too.

V.S. PRITCHETT, *A Cab at the Door*, 1968

UXBRIDGE BRANCH
In peak hours this branch starts at Uxbridge.

Rayners Lane

Early Electric! Maybe even here
    They met that evening at six-fifteen
Beneath the hearts of this electrolier
    And caught the first non-stop to WILLESDEN GREEN,
Then out and on, through rural RAYNER'S LANE
To autumn-scented Middlesex again.

JOHN BETJEMAN, 'The Metropolitan Railway – Baker Street Station Buffet',
A Few Late Chrysanthemums, 1954

South Harrow

There was an old lady of Harrow
Whose views were exceedingly narrow.
    At the end of her paths
    She built two bird baths
For the different sexes of sparrow.

ANON.

Sudbury Hill

Thomas Trollope, father of the novelist, came to Illots Farm Sudbury in 1813–15 and his son used it as a model for 'Orley Farm'.

The London Encyclopaedia edited by Ben Weinreb and Christopher Hibbert, 1983

Sudbury Town

Sir William Perkin, the greatest organic chemist of his time . . . was experimenting in a rough laboratory in his home at Sudbury. Working with his brother on aniline compounds, he discovered the first completely fast mauve dye. It was enthusiastically received by Pullar's of Perth. Within a few months Perkin had opened a small factory at Greenford, and was making dyes in quantity. 'A rage for your colour has set in among that all-powerful class of the community – the ladies,' wrote Pullar; 'if they once take a mania for it and you can supply the demand, your fame and fortune are made.' Mauve was the favourite colour of Queen Victoria – and the fortune was made: Perkin retired at the age of 35 to The Chestnuts, Sudbury. There he devoted himself to research in pure chemistry, to good works and to chamber music.

BRUCE STEVENSON, *Middlesex*, 1972

Alperton

Besides the farmhouses, it comprises a few straggling cottages, with a 'public' [the Chequers] and two or three beershops, along the road by the Grand Junction Canal, and between the canal and little river Brent. It is a pretty summer evening stroll from Sudbury to Twyford and Hanger Hill, across the Alperton meadows, but the brickmaker and the builder threaten a descent upon them.

JAMES THORNE, *Handbook to the Environs of London*, 1876

Park Royal

I remember Park Royal as a little wooden platform, high above the football ground of the Queens Park Rangers and what a pleasant walk one could take by leafy lanes and elmy fields of Middlesex between Preston Road Station on the Metropolitan to the newly electrified Kenton Station on the extension beyond Queens Park of the Bakerloo.

> JOHN BETJEMAN, 'Coffee, Port and Cigars on the Inner Circle',
> *The Times*, 24 May 1963

North Ealing

In the 1890s Ealing was known as 'Queen of the Suburbs'.

Ealing Common
Change for District line

Great Ealing School, second only to the great public schools of Eton and Harrow. . . . In the record of former scholars are men whose names have become household words in every department of English life . . . Thackeray, Newman, Captain Marryat. . . . Huxley's father was a teacher in the school, and undoubtedly Professor Huxley, at an early age, was a scholar, although not for long, as the Huxley family left Ealing when the embryo scientist was only eight years of age.

It is also a matter of note that Louis Philippe, King of the French, was, in the days of his exile, a teacher in the school.

> CHARLES JONES, *Ealing*, 1903

Acton Town
Change for District line

Richard Baxter (the nonconformist divine) decided to leave London, which in any case he says he found deleterious to both health and study:

. . . all Publick Service being at an end, I betook my self to live in the Country (at Acton) that I might set myself to writing, and do what Service I could for Posterity, and live as possibly I could out of the World. Thither I came 1663, July 14. . . .

The Plague which began at *Acton*, July 29 1665 being ceased on March 1 following, I returned home; and found the Church-yard like a plow'd field with Graves, and many of my Neighbours dead; but my

House (near the Church-yard) uninfected, and that part of my Family, which I left there, all safe, thro' the great mercy of God, my merciful Protector.

Of the Great Fire which followed in September he laments especially 'the Loss of Books' as 'an exceeding great Detriment to the Interest of Piety and Learning' and records: 'I saw the half burnt Leaves of Books near my Dwelling at Acton six miles from London but others found them near Windsor, almost twenty miles distant.'

RICHARD BAXTER, *Reliquiae Baxterianae*, 1696

Turnham Green

By the morning of November 13th [1642] the King found his way barred by some 24,000 men drawn up on the broad common of Turnham Green.

W.G. BELL, *Where London Sleeps*, 1926

Great and Bloody News
from
Turnham-Green,
or a
Relation
Of a sharp Encounter
Between the Earl of Pembrook, and his Company,
with the Constable and Watch belonging to the
Parish of Chiswick on the 18 Instant [1680].
In which Conflict Mr Smeethe a Gentleman, and
one Mr Halfpenny a Constable of the said
Parish were mortally Wounded.

W.G. BELL, *Where London Sleeps*, 1926

The most significant suburb built in the last century, probably the most significant in the Western world is Bedford Park, Chiswick [served by Turnham Green Station], laid out in 1876 by Norman Shaw. It was designed specifically for 'artistic people of moderate incomes'. It stands in orchard land and the picturesque brick houses with their faintly Dutch look are late Victorian versions of the small parsonage houses which were built in the heyday of the Gothic revival a generation earlier. . . .

Bedford Park was the origin of many another garden suburb.

> JOHN BETJEMAN, 'The Most Significant Suburb – Bedford Park',
> *Daily Telegraph*, 22 August 1960, quoted in *Betjeman's London*
> edited by Pennie Denton

London Burning! I watched this event from my Chiswick flat last night with disgust and indignation, but with no intensity though the spectacle was superb, I thought. It is nothing like the burning of Troy. Yet the Surrey Docks were ablaze at the back with towers and spires outlined against them, greenish yellow searchlights swept the sky in futile agony, crimson shells burst behind the spire of Turnham Green church. This is all that a world catastrophe amounts to. Something which one is too sad or sullen to appreciate. Perhaps we are really behaving heroically. . . . Someone else will have to say. Now and then tracts of the horizon flashed a ghastly electric green. Or the fire ahead burst up as I hoped it was dying down. Oh! I cried once faintly then returned to my bed and read *Middlemarch*. God help us all. . . . In the morning a crimson valance of cloud hung above the fire itself.

> E.M. FORSTER, 8 September 1940*

*During the Second World War, E.M. Forster lived in No. 9 Arlington Park Mansions, Turnham Green. From his flat he watched the bombing of London's dockland.

Hammersmith
Change for District line and Hammersmith & City line station

So long as Hammersmith is called Hammersmith, its people will live in the shadow of that primal hero, the Blacksmith, who led the democracy of the Broadway into battle till he drove the chivalry of Kensington before him and overthrew them at the place which in honour of the best blood of the defeated aristocracy is still called Kensington Gore.

> G.K. CHESTERTON, *The Napoleon of Notting Hill*, 1904

In the Village of Hammersmith, which was formerly a long scattering Place, full of Gardeners Grounds, with here and there an old House of some Bulk: We see now great Numbers of fine Houses, and a continued Range of great Length, which makes the main Street. A handsome

Square was also begun, but it did not succeed, and the Place is turn'd in to Gardening.

DANIEL DEFOE, *A Tour thro' the Whole Island of Great Britain*, 1738

Barons Court

The Barons Court Estate. This estate was planned by the late Sir William Palliser. The title was devised in allusion to the Court Baron held by the Lord of the Manor, and was, perhaps, suggested to Sir William by the name of the neighbouring district, Earl's Court.

CHARLES JAMES FÈRET, *Fulham Old and New*, 1900

Earl's Court
Change for District line

The tube station is the soul of the place made visible. Around and about it Earl's Court anchors itself. Out of it is disgorged and into it is ingested a steady stream of humanity. A multi-hued, multi-lingual crowd is always gathered near its entrance. Earl's Court is nothing if not cosmopolitan. Long-haired students from the continent weighted under rucksacks studded with the flags of their countries pore over street maps. Bearded Australians study the poster that invites them to join the Zambesi Club – Rhodesians, South Africans, New Zealanders and Canadians also welcome.

SHIVA NAIPAUL in *Living in London* edited by Alan Ross, 1974

Gloucester Road
Change for Circle and District lines

James Barrie, novelist, lived at No. 133 Gloucester Road from 1896 to 1902.

South Kensington
Change for Circle and District lines

Towards five o'clock he [George Forsyte] went out, and took a train at South Kensington Station (for everyone to-day went Underground).

JOHN GALSWORTHY, *The Man of Property*, 1906

As one goes into the South Kensington Art Museum [now the Victoria & Albert] from the Brompton Road, the Gallery of Old Iron is overhead to the right. But the way thither is exceedingly devious and not to be revealed to everybody, since the young people who pursue science and art thereabouts set a peculiar value on its seclusion. The gallery is long and narrow and dark, and set with iron gates, iron-bound chests, locks, bolts, and bars, fantastic great keys, lamps, and the like, and over the balustrade one may lean and talk of one's finer feelings and regard Michael Angelo's horned Moses, or Trajan's Column (in plaster) rising gigantic out of the hall below and far above the level of the gallery.

H.G. WELLS, *Love and Mr Lewisham*, 1900

Knightsbridge

I'm eighteen actually, although
Most people take me for *much* more;
I'm *not* a debutante, you know.
I think it's *such* a bore to go
To parties until three or four.
My father was an aide-de-camp.
We've got an aubergine front door.
I'm *frightfully* keen on Terence Stamp.

I *wish* I had a bigger bust,
Though Mummy says it's frightfully smart
And any more would beckon lust.
She says I absolutely *must*
Stop trying to be keen on art
And dressing like a King's Road tramp.
I simply don't know where to start.
I'm *frightfully* keen on Terence Stamp.

I'm starting on a course quite soon,
It's sort of cookery and flowers.
My latest colour's deep maroon.
And sometimes in the afternoon
I simply lie for hours and hours
Beneath dear Mummy's sun-ray lamp
And contemplate the Carlton Towers.
I'm *frightfully* keen on Terence Stamp.

CANDIDA LYCETT GREEN, 'Knightsbridge Ballade', 1967

. . . the most respectable people have taken to living in neighbour-
hoods which, in my young days, were marshes and grazing meadows
for dairymen's cows, and were at night infested by highwaymen and
footpads. I should like to know where Pagoda Square, Kensington, was
thirty years ago. My dear, Brompton was in the country then, and you
had scarcely passed Hyde Park Corner before you were in the green
lanes. Knightsbridge Green meant something more, in those days, than
a street full of rubbishing little shops.

G.A. SALA, *Lady Chesterfield's Letters to Her Daughter*, 1860

Then, behind, all my hair is done up in a plait,
And so, like a cornet's, tuck'd under my hat,
Then I mount on my palfrey as gay as a lark,
And, follow'd by John, take the dust in Hyde Park.
In the way I am met by some smart macaroni,
Who rides by my side on a little bay pony –
No sturdy Hibernian, with shoulders so wide,
But as taper and slim as the ponies they ride;
Their legs are as slim, and their shoulders no wider,
Dear sweet little creatures, both pony and rider! . . .

In Kensington Gardens to stroll up and down,
You know was the fashion before you left town, . . .

Yet, though 'tis too rural – to come near the mark,
We all herd in *one* walk, and that, nearest the park;
There with ease we may see, as we pass by the wicket,
The chimneys of Knightsbridge, and footmen at cricket.

THOMAS TICKELL (1686–1740), 'On a Woman of Fashion'
quoted in *London Between the Lines* compiled by John Bishop
and Virginia Broadbent, 1973

Hyde Park Corner

Good Mirabell, don't let us be familiar or fond, nor kiss before folks,
like my Lady Fadler and Sir Francis: nor go to Hyde Park together the
first Sunday in a new chariot, to provoke eyes and whispers; and then
never be seen there together again; as if we were proud of one another
the first week, and ashamed of one another ever after. . . . Let us be

very strange and well-bred: let us be as strange as if we had been married a great while; and as well bred as if we were not married at all.

WILLIAM CONGREVE, *The Way of the World*, 1700

Hyde Park, everyone knows, is the promenade of London: nothing was
so much in fashion, during the fine weather, as this promenade, which
was the rendezvous of magnificence and beauty: every one, therefore,
who had either sparkling eyes, or a splendid equipage, constantly
repaired thither; and the king [Charles II] seemed pleased with the
place.

COUNT ANTHONY HAMILTON, *Memoirs of Count Grammont*,
translated with notes by Horace Walpole, with additional notes
and biographical sketches by Sir Walter Scott and
Mrs Ann Jameson, 1888 (first published 1713)

I [Bridget Tisdall] would be wheeled daily into Hyde Park. . . . Here sat
the Balloon Woman with her bunch of balloons and red and yellow
windmills on sticks which the nannies bought for their charges. We
would then cross Rotten Row . . . and turn right into The Daisy Walk
where upper-crust Nannies with crested prams sat knitting, complain-
ing, and generally comparing each other's situations. . . .

The Pryce-Jones Nanny had wheeled herself behind the [Albert]
Memorial and sat down on an empty bench. After a while an older
Nanny appeared, pushing a pram on which was painted a small gold
coronet. She sat down too and they eyed one another. At length the
older Nanny turned to the younger one, coughed, and said 'Excuse
me, Nanny, is your mummy a titled mummy?' 'Actually, no,' said the
Pryce-Jones Nanny.

'You will excuse my mentioning it, Nanny, but this bench is reserved for titled mummies' nannies, Nanny.'

J. GATHORNE-HARDY, *The Rise and Fall of the British Nanny*, 1972

Green Park

Change for Jubilee and Victoria lines

. . . it's dark now, and the long rows of lamps in Piccadilly after dark were beautiful. . . . On the right of that thorough-fare is a row of trees, the railing of the Green Park, and a fine broad eligible piece of pavement.

'Oh, my!' cried Henrietta presently. 'There's been an accident!' I looked to the left, and said, 'Where, Henrietta?'

'Not there, stupid!' said she. 'Over there by the Park railings. Where the crowd is. Oh no, it's not an accident, it's something else to look at! What's them lights?'

She referred to two lights twinkling low amongst the legs of the assemblage: two candles on the pavement.

'Oh, do come along!' cried Henrietta, skipping across the road with me. I hung back, but in vain. 'Do let's look!'

Again, designs upon the pavement. Centre compartment, Mount Vesuvius going it (in a circle), supported by four oval compartments, severally representing a ship in heavy weather, a shoulder of mutton attended by two cucumbers, a golden harvest with distant cottage of proprietor, and a knife and fork after nature; above the centre compartment a bunch of grapes, and over the whole a rainbow. The whole, as it appeared to me, exquisitely done.

CHARLES DICKENS, 'Somebody's Luggage', Christmas Number of
All the Year Round, 1862, reprinted in *Christmas Stories*

. . . *we returned to the station [Green Park] to find that in one of the underground corridors with superb acoustics, Rachel, an attractive lass from St John's Wood, was already deep into the first movement* (Allegro ma non troppo) *of Beethoven's Violin Concerto in D Major with its superb octaval leaps and G-string twiddly bits* staccatissimo. . . . *She was accompanied by a taped orches-*

tral backing known to subterranean maestros as a 'one out', that is with the solo parts professionally erased.

JOHN HILLABY, *John Hillaby's London*, 1987

Piccadilly Circus
Change for Bakerloo line

A pickadil [is] that round hem, or the several divisions set together about the skirt of a Garment, or other thing; also a kinde of stiff collar, made in fashion of a Band. Hence, perhaps the famous Ordinary near St. James, called Pickadilly, took denomination; because it was then the outmost, or skirt house of the Suburbs, that way. Others say it took name from this, that one *Higgins* a Tailor, who built it, got most of his Estate by Pickadilles, which in the last age were much worn in England.

T. BLOUNT, *Glossographia*, 1656

London. I had the first time in my life, a feeling of health. . . . London was indescribably beautiful. The red and brown chimney-pots contrasted so sharply with the blue sky, and all the colours glowed, the gay shops gleamed and the blue air poured out of every cross street and enveloped the background. . . . How beautifully the roses in Piccadilly gleamed in the sunshine, and how full of vitality everything seemed. It gave me a strange but very comforting sensation and I felt the power of returning health. I shall bring away very dear memories of this town, and when I drive off on the stage-coach. . . . I shall look back many a time and think of the pleasure I have had here.

FELIX MENDELSSOHN, letter to his family, 6 November 1829

I remember an evening at the Café Royal (can we grey beards *never* set pen to paper without remembering some evening at the Café Royal?) when Oscar Wilde, who had for some time been talking in a vein of iridescent nonsense about some important matter, paused and said, with good reason and with genuine feeling, 'My dear Will [Rothenstein], don't look so serious!'

MAX BEERBOHM, *A Peep into the Past and Other Prose Pieces*
collected by Rupert Hart-Davis, 1972

There, on that October evening – there, in that exuberant vista of gilding and crimson velvet set amidst all those opposing mirrors and upholding caryatids, with fumes of tobacco ever rising to the painted and pagan ceiling, and with the turn of presumably cynical conversation broken into so sharply now and again by a clatter of dominoes shuffled on marble tables, I drew a deep breath and 'This indeed,' said I to myself, 'is life'.

MAX BEERBOHM, describing his first visit to the Café Royal,
Piccadilly, with William Rothenstein

It's a long way to Tipperary, it's a long way to go;
It's a long way to Tipperary, to the sweetest girl I know!
Goodbye Piccadilly, farewell Leicester Square;
It's a long long way to Tipperary, but my heart's right there!

HARRY WILLIAMS AND JACK JUDGE, 1908

Leicester Square
Change for Northern line

. . . in 1783 he [John Hunter, the founder of the Royal College of Surgeons] took a house upon a much larger scale, in Leicester Square, about the middle of the eastern side, which extended through, into Castle-Street. This was fitted up in a very expensive manner; – and here he established an expansive room for his Museum, – another for a public medical levee, on every Sunday evening, another for a lyceum for medical disputation, – another for his course of lectures; another for dissection, – another for a printing warehouse and a press, – and another for reading his medical works. . . .

. . . Soon as he was settled in this new house, he sent out cards of invitation to those of the faculty, his selection suggested, – to attend on Sunday evenings, during the winter months, at his levee; and they

were regaled, with tea and coffee, and treated with medical occurrences.
JESSE FOOT, *The Life of John Hunter,* 1794

Covent Garden

1752. One night when Beauclerk and Langton had supped at a tavern
in London, and sat till about three in the morning, it came into their
heads to go and knock up Johnson, and see if they could prevail on
him to join them in a ramble. They rapped violently at the door of his
chambers in the Temple, till at last he appeared in his shirt, with his little black wig on the top of his head, instead of a nightcap, and a poker
in his hand, imagining, probably, that some ruffians were coming to
attack him. When he discovered who they were, and was told their
errand, he smiled, and with great good-humour agreed to their propo-
sal: 'What, is it you, you dogs! I'll have a frisk with you.' He was soon
drest, and they sallied forth together into Covent Garden . . .

JAMES BOSWELL, *The Life of Samuel Johnson,* 1791

I have been apprised several times during the night that this was a
market morning in Covent Garden. I have seen waggons surmounted
by enormous mountains of vegetable baskets wending their way
through the silent streets. I have been met by the early costermongers
in their donkey-carts, and chaffed by the costerboys on my forlorn
appearance. But I have reserved Covent Garden as a *bonne bouche* – a
wind-up to my pilgrimage; for I have heard and read how fertile is the
market in question in subjects of amusement and contemplation.

I confess that I am disappointed. Covent Garden seems to me to be
but one great accumulation of cabbages. I am pelted with these vegeta-
bles as they are thrown from the lofty summits of piled waggons to
costermongers standing at the base. I stumble among them as I walk;
in short, above, below, on either side, cabbages preponderate.

G.A. SALA, *Papers Humorous and Pathetic,* 1872

. . . a boy being born on St George's Day, 1775, began soon after to
take interest in the world of Covent Garden, and put to service such
spectacles of life as it afforded.

. . . Besides men and women, dusty sunbeams up or down the street
on summer mornings; deep furrowed cabbage-leaves at the green-
grocer's; magnificence of oranges . . . ; wheelbarrows round the

corner; and Thames' shore within three minutes' race. . . .

His foregrounds had always a succulent cluster or two of greengrocery at the corners. Enchanted oranges gleam in Covent Gardens of the Hesperides; and great ships go to pieces in order to scatter chests of them on the waves.

> JOHN RUSKIN on J.M.W. Turner's boyhood,
> *Modern Painters*, Part IX, 1860

Of ballet fans we are the cream,
  We never miss a night;
The ballet is our only theme,
Our Russian accent is a dream,
We say the name of every prim
  A *ballerina* right;
The ballet is our meat and drink,
  It is our staff of life,
Our prop, our safety valve, our link,
Our vice, our passion, foible, kink,
The ballet is,
We really think,
  Our mistress and our wife.

It's true that many lesser clans
  For ballet also thirst,
But they are merely *nouveau* fans,
  It's we who liked it first,
And we who know it best, becos,
  Ask any *connoisseur*,
The ballet isn't what it was
  When we were what we were.
    Oh, the urge
    To see Serge!
    What a thrill!
    What a pill!
    What a purge!
    So adept
    When he leapt,
    We were dumb,
    Overcome,
    Overswept!

> HERBERT FARJEON, 'When Bolonsky Danced Belushka',
> *Nine Sharp and Earlier*, 1938

The phantom of William Terriss, a famous leading man of the 1890s, also prefers to haunt in winter. He visits Covent Garden Underground Station as well as the Adelphi Theatre where he was appearing at the time of his violent death. An account of an appearance of his ghost was printed in the *Sunday Dispatch* on 15 January 1956:

Who is the ghost of Covent Garden Underground Station? Some people believe the station is haunted by a Victorian actor.

A four-page report has been sent to the London Transport Executive divisional headquarters. And this question has been put to officials:

Is the statuesque figure wearing white gloves and seen by members of the station staff, the spectre of William Terriss, the actor stabbed to death at the Adelphi Theatre by a maniac 59 years ago? . . .

Just after midnight last November the last passenger had left the platform. Foreman Collector Jack Hayden saw a tall distinguished-looking man go into the exit.

'Catch that man coming up the emergency stairs, Bill,' he phoned the booking clerk. *But no one was there.*

J.A. BROOKS, *Ghosts of London*, 1982

Aldwych
Now closed

The Aldwych branch of the Piccadilly from Holborn was closed on 21 September 1940 and it stayed closed throughout the war, re-opening on 1 July 1946. Many British Museum treasures, including the Elgin Marbles, spent the war in the Aldwych branch tunnels.

JOHN R. DAY, *The Story of London's Underground*, 1963

Holborn
Change for Central line

GLOUCESTER:

My Lord of Ely, when I was last in Holborn,
I saw good strawberries in your garden there;
I do beseech you send for some of them.

ELY:

Marry, and will, my Lord, with all my heart.

WILLIAM SHAKESPEARE, *Richard III*, 1593

. . . a brook 'as clear as crystal' once ran right down Holborn, when Turnstile really was a turnstile leading slap away into the meadows.

CHARLES DICKENS, *Bleak House*, 1852–3

When I am sad and weary
When I think all hope is gone
When I walk along High Holborn
I think of you with nothing on.

ADRIAN MITCHELL, 'Celia Celia', *Adrian Mitchell: Greatest Hits*, 1991

Russell Square

. . . his bedroom window looked out on a south-west garden-wall, covered with flowering jessamine through June and July. There had been roses, too, in this London garden. Gray must always have flowers about him, and he trudged down to Covent Garden every day, for his sweet peas and pinks, scarlet martagon lilies, double stocks and flowering marjoram. His drawing-room looked over Bedford Gardens, and a fine stretch of upland fields, crowned at last against the sky by the villages of Highgate and Hampstead . . . he is working every day at the Museum, feasting upon literary plums and walnuts.

EDMUND GOSSE, *Gray*, 1882, describing Thomas Gray's (1716–71) lodgings near Russell Square, where he had come to study in the newly opened British Museum

He sat in the Underground train to Russell Square. Before anything

else he must get back his Reading Room ticket. That was his true iden-
tity card.

MAUREEN DUFFY, *Capital*, 1975

What? Russell Square!
There's lilac there!
And Torrington
And Woburn Square
Intrepid don
The season's wear.
In Gordon Square and Euston Square –
There's lilac, there's laburnum there!
In green and gold and lavender
Queen Square and Bedford Square,
All Bloomsbury and all Soho
With every sunbeam gayer grow,
Greener grow and gayer.

JOHN DAVIDSON, 'Laburnum and Lilac',
Pall Mall Magazine, 1906

King's Cross St. Pancras

Change for Circle, Hammersmith & City, Metropolitan, Northern
and Victoria lines

O Time, bring back those midnights and those friends,
Those glittering moments that a spirit lends,
That all may be imagined from the flash,
The cloud-hit god-game through the lightning gash,
Those hours of stricken sparks from which men took
Light to send out to men in song or book;
Those friends who heard St. Pancras's bells strike two,
Yet stayed until the barber's cockerel crew,
Talking of noble styles, the Frenchman's best,
And thought beyond great poets not expressed,
The glory of mood where human frailty failed,
The forts of human light not yet assailed.

JOHN MASEFIELD, 'Biography', *Collected Poems*, 1923

Caledonian Road

A work-basket made of an old armadillo
  Lined with pink satin now rotten with age,
A novel entitled *The Ostracized Vicar*
  (A spider squashed flat on the title-page),
A faded album of nineteen-oh-seven
  Snapshots (now like very weak tea)
Showing high-collared knuts and girls expectant
  In big muslin hats at Bexhill-on-Sea,
A gasolier made of hand-beaten copper
  In the once modern style known as *art nouveau*
An assegai, and a china slipper,
  And *What a Young Scoutmaster Ought to Know*.

Who stood their umbrellas in elephants' feet?
  Who hung their hats on the horns of a moose?
Who crossed the ocean with amulets made
  To be hung round the neck of an ailing papoose?
Who paid her calls with a sandalwood card-case?
  From whose eighteen-inch waist hung that thin châtelaine?
Who smoked that meerschaum? Who won that medal?
  That extraordinary vase was evolved by what brain?
Who worked in wool the convolvulus bell-pull?
  Who smiled with those false teeth? Who wore that wig?
Who had that hair tidy hung by her mirror?
  Whose was the scent-bottle shaped like a pig? . . .

Laugh if you like at this monstrous detritus
  Of middle-class life in the liberal past,
The platypus stuffed, and the frightful épergne.
  You who are now overtaxed and declassed,
Laugh while you can, for the time may come round
  When the rubbish you treasure will lie in this place –
Your wireless set (bust), your ridiculous hats,
  And the photographs of your period face.
Your best-selling novels, your 'functional' chairs,
  Your primitive comforts and notions of style
Are just so much fodder for dealers in junk
  Let us hope that they'll make your grandchildren smile.

WILLIAM PLOMER, 'The Caledonian Market', *Selected Poems*, 1940

*The Cyclopean eye of the advancing train, the adventure of boarding, the fastid-
iousness in the choice of a neighbour, the sense of equality, the mysterious and
flattering reflection of oneself in the opposite windows, even of the colours of the
various stations – from the orange and lemon of Covent Garden to the bistre
melancholy of Caledonian Road or Camden Town, faint cerulean like an
autumnal sky.*

COMPTON MACKENZIE (?), 1933 (?)

Holloway Road

The new lumber of a London-going dray,
The still-new stucco on the London clay,
Hot summer silence over Holloway.

JOHN BETJEMAN quoted in *Betjeman Country*
by Frank Delaney, 1985

. . . Crane Grove Secondary, up past Highbury Corner, off the
Holloway Road. The five- and six-storey schools in this part stand
above the three-storey streets like chaotic castellations. Dead cinemas
and a music hall sadden corners, abandoned. Only Arsenal stadium,
older-looking in its outdated modernity than last century's houses,
competes in height with the dark red brick, stonedressed schools.
Swart sleek diesels shaped as functionally as otters pass and re-pass
solemnly between strips of houses at eaves-level pulling trains of rust-
stained waggons.

B.S. JOHNSON, *Albert Angelo*, 1964

Arsenal

The story of Islington's favourite football club in fact begins in
Woolwich in the days of the first soccer boom, when as yet there was
more enthusiasm for rugger than soccer in the south. The Scots then
working at Woolwich Arsenal wanted to redress the balance by setting
up a football team. David Danskin managed to get 15 signatures per 6d
a time but he had to add a further 10s.6d from his own pocket to buy a
soccer ball.

Originally the team, founded in the autumn of 1886, was known as
Dial Square after the particular set of workshops from which most of
the players were drawn. From the first the colours of the team were

scarlet. . . . Subsequently as the fame of the team spread and the rumour went around that the key to a job at the Arsenal was the ability to play football well the name was changed first to Woolwich Arsenal . . . and subsequently when the club moved its headquarters to Highbury in 1913 it became commonsense to drop the Woolwich part of the title.

SONIA ROBERTS, *The Story of Islington*, 1975

The thirties were a good decade for the team: they won their first FA Cup in 1930, and in the course of the decade were league champions five times. Their glory was celebrated in the renaming of Gillespie Road Underground station [to Arsenal]. They won their first League and FA Cup double in 1970/71.

ANN USBORNE, *A Portrait of Islington*, 1981

Finsbury Park
Change for Victoria line

The train, though it did not start for an hour, was already drawn up at the end of the platform, and he lay down in it and slept. With the first jolt he was in daylight; they had left the gateways of King's Cross, and were under blue sky. Tunnels followed, and after each the sky grew bluer, and from the embankment at Finsbury Park he had his first sight of the sun. It rolled along behind the eastern smokes – a wheel, whose fellow was the descending moon – and as yet it seemed the servant of the blue sky, not its lord.

E.M. FORSTER, *Howards End*, 1910

Not long ago, at the height of the rush hour, I was strap-hanging, and in that half of the carriage, that is, among fourteen people, three people read books among all the newspapers. In the morning, off to work, people betray their allegiances: The Times, *the* Independent, *the* Guardian, *the* Telegraph, *the* Mail. . . . *At night the* Evening Standard *adds itself to the display. Three people. At my right elbow a man was reading the* Iliad. *Across the aisle a woman read* Moby Dick. *As I pushed out, a girl held up* Wuthering Heights *over the head of a new baby asleep on her chest.*

The poem holding its own among the advertisements was:

INFANT JOY

DORIS LESSING, 'In Defence of the Underground', *London Observed*, 1992

Manor House

Manor House. Close by the station stands the Manor House public house. Known as the 'Manor Tavern' when it was built in *c.*1820 as a stopping place for travellers between London and Cambridge.

CYRIL M. HARRIS, *What's in a Name?*, 1977

Turnpike Lane

The Turnpike gate, which was erected in 1767, was removed in the 1870s.

For my part, now, I consider supper as a turnpike, through which one must pass in order to get to bed. 17 April 1778.

J. BOSWELL, *The Life of Samuel Johnson*, 1791

Wood Green

Wood Green has a history as a rural hamlet originating in a small settlement at the foot of a wooded hill in the heart of which was a green. . . . Today it is best known for its shopping city, a complex designed by Richard, Sheppard, Robson and Partners which took seven years to build and was officially opened by the Queen on 13 May 1981.

The London Encyclopaedia edited by Ben Weinreb and Christopher Hibbert, 1983

Bounds Green

Bounds Green . . . name is derived from its association with the families of John le Bonde in 1294 and Walter le Bounde during the 13th century . . . recorded as Le boundes in 1365.

CYRIL M. HARRIS, *What's in a Name?*, 1977

Arnos Grove

The largest oak in this district [in Middlesex], known as the Minchenden oak, is at Arno's Grove, Southgate. It is said to have the widest spread of branches of any English oak. This oak, then termed the Chandos oak, is figured in Strutt's *Sylvia*, and also in Loudon's *Arboretum*. The latter gives the branch spread as having an overall diameter of 118 feet, and the girth, one foot from the ground, as 18 ft. 3 in.

The Victoria History of the County of Middlesex edited by William Page, 1911

DEVELOPMENT ACT 1929
PICCADILLY RAILWAY
Southgate Extension from Finsbury Park
STATION SITE
suggested names
ARNOS GROVE   ARNOS PARK   SOUTHGATE
Write and tell us what name you suggest.

Large notice outside the original Arnos Grove station

Southgate

. . . it is a pleasure to me to know that I was even born in so sweet a village as Southgate. I first saw the light there on the 19th of October 1784. It found me cradled, not only in the lap of the nature which I love, but in the midst of the truly English scenery which I love beyond all other. Middlesex in general . . . is a scene of trees and meadows, of 'greenery' and nestling cottages; and Southgate is a prime specimen of Middlesex. It is a place lying out of the way of innovation, therefore it has the pure, sweet air of antiquity about it.

LEIGH HUNT, *Autobiography*, 1850

Oakwood

Oakwood station is decorated with the coat of arms showing stags heads and a Latin motto alleging that oak trees grow from acorns. But as well as the rural fictions of heraldry there are proper country trees beside the track waving their branches wildly in the south-west wind.

PHILIP HOWARD, *The Times*

Cockfosters

. . . few except the natives ever take the golden road to Cockfosters and the other terminal stations of Underground lines.

PHILIP HOWARD, *The Times*

So she spent the next three hours doing what she always did when she was on her own in the holidays. She rode on the London Transport trains. Sitting on a Piccadilly Line train which she picked up at King's Cross, she travelled to Cockfosters, at the end of the line. She would have liked to get out of the station and see the place, but that wasn't possible. She had only her imagination to give her a picture of what Cockfosters might look like. Jass imagined the sort of country she liked best. Soft, grassy hills, folding into each other as far as you could see. Perhaps an old farmhouse, with yellow lichen on the roof.

CATHERINE STORR, *The Underground Conspiracy*, 1987

ACKNOWLEDGEMENTS

We would like to thank our families and friends who have helped us over the years during the preparation of this book, especially Sandy Marriage, Robin Ollington, Bryan Rooney, Suzanne St Albans, Anthony Sampson, Kathleen Tillotson, Malcolm Holmes of the Camden Local History Library and the staff of the North Reading Room, British Library.

The compilers and publishers gratefully acknowledge permission to reproduce the following copyright material in this book:

Max Beerbohm: *A Peep into the Past.* © Max Beerbohm 1972. Reprinted by permission of Mrs Reichmann.

John Betjeman: 'The Metropolitan Railway – Baker Street Station Buffet' (*A Few Late Chrysanthemums* 1954), from *Collected Poems.* © John Betjeman 1958. Reprinted by permission of John Murray.

J.A. Brooks: *Ghosts of London*, © J.A. Brooks 1982. Reprinted by permission of Jarrold Publishing.

Frank Delaney: *Betjeman Country*, © Frank Delaney 1983. Reprinted by permission of Hodder & Stoughton.

Pennie Denton (ed.): *Betjeman's London*, © Pennie Denton 1988. Reprinted by permission of John Murray.

Maureen Duffy: *Capital*, © Maureen Duffy 1975. Reprinted by permission of Jonathan Cape.

H. Farjeon: 'When Bolonsky Danced Belushka' from *Nine Sharp and Earlier*, © H. Farjeon 1938. Reprinted by permission of David Higham Associates and the Estate of Herbert Farjeon.

E.M. Forster: *Howard's End*, © E.M. Forster 1910. Reprinted by permission of King's College, Cambridge and The Society of Authors as the literary representatives of the E.M. Forster Estate.

Candida Lycett Green: 'Knightsbridge Ballade', © Candida Lycett Green 1967. Reprinted by permission of Candida Lycett Green.

John Hillaby: *John Hillaby's London*, © John Hillaby 1987. Reprinted by permission of Constable.

Philip Howard: 'Wapping' and 'Philip Howard looks at London' from *The Times*, © Times Newspapers. Reeprinted by permission of Times Newspapers.

ACKNOWLEDGEMENTS

B.S. Johnson: *Albert Angelo*, © B.S. Johnson 1964. Reprinted by permission of Constable.

Doris Lessing: 'In Defence of the Underground' from *London Observed: Stories and Sketches*, © Doris Lessing 1992. Reprinted in an abridged form by permission of Jonathan Clowes on behalf of Doris Lessing, published by HarperCollins.

Christopher Logue: 'Last Night in London Airport' from *Ode to the Dodo: Poems 1953–1978*, © Christopher Logue 1981, published by Jonathan Cape. Reprinted by permission of Christopher Logue.

John Masefield: 'Biography' from *Collected Poems*, © John Masefield 1923. Reprinted by permission of The Society of Authors as literary representatives of the Estate of John Masefield.

Adrian Mitchell: 'Celia Celia' from *Adrian Mitchell: Greatest Hits*, © Adrian Mitchell 1991. Reproduced by permission of Bloodaxe Books.

Shiva Naipaul: in *Living in London* edited by Alan Ross, © Shiva Naipaul 1974. Reprinted by permission of London Magazine.

William Plomer: 'The Caledonian Market' from *Selected Poems*, © William Plomer 1940. Reprinted by permission of The Hogarth Press.

Margaret and Alick Potter: *Everything is Possible*, © M. and A. Potter 1984. Reprinted by permission of Margaret and Alick Potter, published by Alan Sutton.

V.S. Pritchett: *A Cab at the Door*, © V.S. Pritchett 1968. Reprinted by permission of Chatto & Windus.

Bruce Stevenson: *Middlesex*, © Bruce Stevenson 1972. Reprinted by permission of B.T. Batsford.

Catherine Storr: *The Underground Conspiracy*, © Catherine Storr 1987. Reprinted by permission of Peters, Fraser & Dunlop.

Anne Usborne: *A Portrait of Islington*, © Ann Usborne 1981, 1989. Reprinted by permission of Damien Tunnacliffe.

Ben Weinreb and Christopher Hibbert: *The London Encyclopaedia*, © Ben Weinreb and Christopher Hibbert 1983. Reprinted by permission of Macmillan London.

H.G. Wells: *Love and Mr Lewisham*, © H.G. Wells 1900. Reprinted by permission of A.P. Watt on behalf of The Literary Executors of the Estate of H.G. Wells.

The publishers have made every effort to contact copyright holders where they can be found. The publishers will be happy to include any missing copyright acknowledgements in future editions.